PRESENCE
AND
STRUCTURE

PRESENCE
AND
STRUCTURE
A Reflection on
Celebration, Worship, and Faith

by
Anthony T. Padovano

PAULIST PRESS
New York, N.Y. / Paramus, N.J.

Library of Congress
Catalog Card Number: 75-32107

ISBN: 0-8091-1912-9

Published by Paulist Press
Editorial Office: 1865 Broadway, N.Y., N.Y. 10023
Business Office: 400 Sette Drive, Paramus, N.J. 07652

Printed and bound in the
United States of America

CONTENTS

1

PRESENCE

The important realities of life are simple. And so it is with worship. Someone is present and we turn to him. People who love each other never choose to turn the other way. Worship is what we do when we sense the presence of someone we do not want to miss.

Many of our fellowmen have considered worship useless, even harmful. For Immanuel Kant, the philosopher, worship was fanaticism and superstition. Others see a value in worship but do not care about whether they worship or not. In this book, we shall be concerned with the reasons why many intelligent and mature people have found in worship some of the richest experiences in human living.

We know from our own lives that nothing is more treasured than the nearness of those we care for and the gratitude we retain for all that they are. Worship derives from this experience. It is rooted in the reality and mystery of presence.

We do not worship if we sense no one is there or if we care little about his being there. Worship is a worthwhile experience precisely because it is directed toward someone else. It has persisted in history because it is an intimate element in the process by which we become human. It is as necessary to

1

human development as the need to grow sensitive toward others, a need that worship seeks to meet. Unless the mystery of presence is appreciated on many levels, one worships at a disadvantage if not in vain. This may be why Jesus expected us to end our anger with our brother before we came to the altar with our gift.

We are acquainted with many instances of the difference the mystery of presence makes in our personal lives. A child in a hospital responds to the grace of his mother's presence more profoundly than he does to medicine or even surgery. A friend at the funeral of someone we love supports us by his nearness. We attend the wedding of a brother so that our being there may increase his joy. A father's hand on the shoulder of his son gives courage and strength. The presence of others heals us and makes us grateful for life. We plan parties and offer gifts so that others may know we think of them and love them, need them and want them.

One values worship in direct proportion to the worth he assigns the mystery of presence. Contemporary culture exaggerates man's role as builder or worker, his contribution to social or political tasks. Worship seeks his presence, not his usefulness in a competitive economic system. In this sense, it resists those who disregard the worth of human life unless it fits into their schemes.

Worship emerges naturally from a heart filled with life; it is the ritual expression of a spirit sensitive to presence. Worship is suffocated by an age that prefers machines and values products more than people. Worship depends on the way we deal with one another. It derives from victories over prejudice and pettiness. It is rooted in life-style and human relationships.

Many worship today as an obligation, an imperative, something they must do. This might lead us to suppose that worship begins with fear. Some believe religious history is little more than a catalogue of fears with intermittent deficiencies in maturity. It is easy to overlook the fact that supposedly primitive cultures exaggerate rather than denigrate the mystery of presence. They see everything inhabited by a personal presence which they name and attempt to encounter. Ritual and tribal dance do not witness to fear but rather to belief in cosmic presence and community awareness.

Why is it, then, that obligation is often associated with worship? Obligation begins as the tribe formalizes its worship and compels people to celebrate that which they have not yet experienced. We who come on the scene late perceive the unfortunate results of a wonderful and fascinating process. We find it perhaps as irrelevant as the person who learns the name of someone whose life holds no interest for him.

Life is most exciting and human when we trace it to its sources and uncover its roots. That is what we shall attempt in the present work. We assume that our ancestors would not have given time and solemnity to worship unless it once was an exciting experience. Nothing is more soul-stirring than meeting another person, discovering in someone else not only one's identity but also a life that is not ours, but to which we are, in some strange way, inseparably bound.

Worship begins when persons meet, when they

need to know each other's names, when they seek words to bind them more closely. To recognize those to whom we belong is an indispensable ingredient in our identity. To find in others the roots and origins of our own life, to grasp in some way the mystery of love and the names of those who gave us life is a discovery of expectation and reverence. Some seek in life a greater grace, a deeper mystery, an indestructible universal love before whom they stand or kneel in wonder.

It is not only recognizing those to whom we belong but being recognized by them that we require. The inability or refusal by those we love to receive us as their own is tragic. This theme is frequently dramatized and most often with unerring success. One never sees such a performance without realizing how destructive an experience of this kind would be for himself. Each of us is scarred and bruised unless he finds love in his origins and until he is loved by those he recognizes as essential to his existence.

All religious behavior is explainable in terms of human experience. We do not mean by this that religious behavior is the same as human experience or measured only by it. We mean that human situations begin a process that sooner or later terminate in religious expression. An effective teacher is capable of explaining a religious phenomenon in the familiar categories of life.

Worship is an endeavor at recognition, a journey of belonging, a way of returning home. It is the search for a familiar face, begun in the hope we shall hear our names spoken by someone whose name we seek to learn through love. There is pity in the fact that for many, worship is sterile, empty, routine, deadening.

A harbor has little meaning for those who see it from the shore. Its meaning is reserved for those who have undertaken a voyage and suffered the terror of exposure, the possibility they might be no more should the angry sea or a contrary wind undo them before they anchor in safety. The reform of the liturgy and the renewal of the Church have pushed us from the shore so that we might experience the process that made worship what it is and so that we might color it with the texture of our own search in danger and hope to a harbor, a home, and a Father.

We mentioned in the beginning the fact that an attitude that makes more of machines than people will assign no value to worship. Such an attitude also makes devotion elusive. One can devote himself only to persons. An impersonal world of machinery and technology, a world that prizes consumer products more than real relationships, a world more anxious about its economic than its human structures, will be a world that cares not for devotion or commitment, fidelity or sacrifice.

Machines do not respond to the offer of ourselves. Involvement is kept to the minimum of proper functioning when a machine is operating. When people are employed for their usefulness, one measures the worth of a person by income or assets, titles or power. Yet those who reach the top of their respective endeavors are often aware of how much accident and chance *was* involved in their success and of how easily a thousand others might have been where they are. Even in terms of talent, arbitrary standards of measurement remain arbitrary.

If we approach liturgy with these unfortunate attitudes, worship becomes as plastic and contrived as the world view of those who depersonalize reality

by their mechanistic manipulation of it. Worship becomes as rigid as a piece of machinery, solid perhaps but with none of the flexibility, the give-and-take of a living reality. There is seldom more than one way to operate a machine properly; for some people, worship is equally unbending and unyielding. They celebrate in a wooden and contrived manner.

It has been said that only human beings have a sense of humor. Animals do not laugh. The more human one's life becomes, the more humor he expresses. We do not mean by "humor" silliness. We mean a capacity to handle life with deftness and grace, without heaviness or intensity. Emotional illness is often indicated by a lack of humor precisely because the world of the mentally disturbed person becomes less personal; it seems threatened on every side by dark and dire forces.

Worship has the capacity to restore one's humor by the grace of presence it celebrates. Its intent is to make the world not so much a mechanized universe or a rational construct or a reality governed by inflexible and impersonal laws. Rather, it encounters at the heart of the world a God who gives and takes so that he is one reality, personal in every way yet distinct in three relationships. The Father is not inflexible but yields to the Son. Worship confesses that even death is not inflexible but gives way to further life. Worship marks the seasons of the year with life; it tempers winter and personalizes spring with the mystery of Christ. It reminds us that God has a sense of humor and that salvation begins with the gentleness of infancy, the deftness of angelic song, and the gracefulness of shepherds in the field.

Worship tends not only to the glory of God but

to the worth of man. It forever tells man he is not a machine, that he is human, and that he alone of all the creatures of the earth can involve himself in a liturgy of love. It leads him to do something that has no measurable value so that he might realize there is something immeasurable about himself. Worship yields to no rational analysis, for man is more significant than reason.

We have described worship in this chapter as a meeting of many concerns and values. The way we worship tells us a great deal about the way we live. The important realities of life are simple, we said in the opening paragraph. Worship is most human when it is most simple. As the world becomes less human, it becomes more complicated. God is simple, not complicated, because God is the core of reality, the mystery we cannot grasp not because he is difficult to comprehend but because we are not simple enough to perceive him.

The Gospel is a simple message, direct, not easy to miss, neither convoluted nor intricate. People live by the most simple experiences. Love is simple; hate is complicated. Hatred leads to opaque and obscure thinking; love is spontaneous, neither planned nor programed. The important realities of life are simple because everyone must share them to be human. They must be available to a child and to an elderly person, to the unlettered and to the informed, to those who are thoughtless and to those who think too much.

A complicated liturgy would not only reach fewer people, it would also be a sign that the Church had lost its humanity. Christian worship is most effective in its simple elements and open gestures. It is

an ensemble of water and wine, of oil and bread, of hands that touch and bless, of anointings and washings. All understand these realities because we live by them. Worship deals with flowers and candles, with light and shepherd staffs, with coals that burn and scents that fill the air, with colored vestments and festive music, with arms that offer peace and dance that rings the world with joy.

2
WORDS AND SYMBOLS

Love requires that people talk to each other sooner or later. In fact, love makes people express themselves, for love is a donation of self as well as an acceptance of another.

Christians believe that even in God a Word is required so that a Spirit of Love may form a Trinity. No love occurs without words. Those whose mental deficiencies or physical handicaps do not allow the use of a language as we know it strive to come as close as possible to the mystery of the word.

Love is a verbal experience. It is the most intense and enriching of all verbal experiences. One never says as much as he does when he speaks of love. Son and father, brother and sister, husband and wife, God and man are relationships in which language bears more meaning than in any other situation. In these relationships, words heal or bruise, transform or demean more effectively, offer or reject more decisively than in the more frequent but less significant use of everyday language.

Christianity emphasizes the value of words more than any other major religion. The Son is the Word in the Trinity. The Incarnation is the Word become human. The Scripture is the Word of God. Christian worship begins with the liturgy of the Word. Faith, St. Paul insists, comes from preaching;

and, preaching is an essentially verbal ministry. Mary receives an angelic message and God's love by accepting: "Let it be according to your word." A venerable Catholic prayer describes the result of this submission: "And the Word was made flesh to dwell with us."

Words are also weapons of incalculable evil. Satan is called "father" but he is not the Father of the Word. He is the father of lies. The reverse of speaking is not silence since silence can also communicate. The reverse of speaking is lying since lies communicate not presence but its absence. The misuse of words leads to a kingdom, the kingdom of darkness; the service of love in words leads to another kingdom, the kingdom of light.

The need to hear the truth, to be given the right words, to breathe in an atmosphere of honesty is a profound human requirement. We say in English that a man of honor is one who keeps his word. The same reality is often capable of radically different results. The kiss in Gethsemane might have been a greeting. The words that make love happen can be used to engender hate. The words that lead people to trust one another can be instantly converted into destructiveness. Words can take us on the wrong journey and so criss-cross with deception the road we follow that eventually we lose the way.

Sometimes words are used in a more complicated manner. They do not bring life directly or take it away. They constitute a paradox, a two-edged sword. They cause pain so that further life may happen. Words may be used prophetically. Liturgy and preaching often seek such words. Prophetic words cause a kind of death to occur, but the purpose of

this death is not the destruction of the person but his growth. The prophet never prefers the pain he causes. He accepts its inevitability with a heavy heart. But he will not allow himself the comfort of not assuming this necessary ministry. There may be death in his words, but because of his love and the truth he speaks, life does not end.

Prophetic communication does not occur only on the formal level we have described. As with all religious realities, it is present in some way in everyday life. A father may be compelled to disturb the illusions on which his son is building his life; a friend may complain about the greed or vindictiveness he sees in another; a sister may counsel her brother about his materialism; a teacher may resist a student's narrowness. These instances of prophetic communication cause pain and yet they are motivated by love and seek more life. Sometimes people use the excuse of giving good advice or of being prophetic merely to meddle or to harm or to dominate. The test of the difference lies in the fact that the meddler loves to interfere. A prophet is always reluctant to say what he has to say.

When prophetic communication is formal and Christian, it derives directly from the New Testament. The prophet, however, does not apply the New Testament rigidly to fluid human situations or changing times. The prophet suffers not only from the message he bears and from the fact that he would rather have others speak it, he suffers also the resistance of those he seeks to help. The anger they feel at the death of their former comfort is often directed at the prophet to destroy him and silence his message. This is the fate Jesus Christ endures.

In different ways, we attest to the power words exercise. We take time and think carefully about the names we give children. When Pope John XXIII conversed with Premier Nikita Khruschev's daughter, he asked the names of her children. She answered and then asked why he inquired. He observed that he enjoyed hearing a mother speak the names of her children because she said those words the way she said no others.

To bestow a name is a significant action. Conversely, we tend to be hesitant to give our name to someone else. We would think little of telling a stranger the time of day or the best way to arrive at a certain destination. We might comment about the weather to a passenger on a bus or train. We might even give an opinion to someone taking a survey. In all these instances, however, we might refuse to give our name or pause a moment to consider before deciding to do so. Centuries ago, people were even more reluctant. In Homer's *Odyssey*, the hero is not asked and does not give his name for some days after living in the homes of those whose hospitality he accepts. The Jewish Scriptures attest to the great favor God grants his people by entrusting them with the knowledge of his name. And yet, as one thinks of it, a name is but a word.

The power words have over us is demonstrated by how often we request people not to say certain things or by the effort we make to keep some people from talking. On other occasions, we ask people to speak to us, to aid us by their voice, to console us not only with their presence but by their words.

Words play a prominent part in the process of worship. Sometimes there may be silence in worship

but more often words are used. Indeed, silence is not meaningful between persons until they have shared words. One may be silent beside an unknown passenger on a plane but this silence has no meaning because there has been no previous and significant verbal communication. The silence of a mother, however, as she proudly watches her son graduate or the silence of a wife who has prayed with her husband is different.

The most frightening of human experiences is the silence of rejection. When people decide they no longer wish to share words they indicate a lack of human interest in each other. Silence can be unsettling in even relatively trivial relationships. We would be angry, feel foolish and rejected if we inquired about the most direct route to a particular location and the one we asked walked away without speaking a word. Silence shatters when we reveal to another the deepest needs or the most ardent hopes of our lives and they refuse to respond. This is the silence of death, of despair, of divorce.

William Carlos Williams, the American poet, observed that divorce is the sign of our times. Connections and communion between persons is elusive. Words are one of the healing influences that can build bridges of communication.

Worship is linked with the mystery of presence, as we know. Words are presence in another form. We recall the presence of another by the words we remember. We may repeat the words of someone who has died or is absent to retain his presence. Most of us are gratified when people tell us they have not forgotten words we shared with them on certain occasions. We become impatient at our in-

ability to articulate at times because our presence to others seems limited, unrealized. When we are angry with someone we close our ears to his or her voice. In these instances, we perceive the relationship between words and presence.

Although words play such an extraordinary role in human life, there are times when they are not sufficient. The more profound emotions become, the more difficult it is to verbalize them. What do we do when we cannot say what we experience? The most instinctive response to this predicament is signs or symbols. A person who can no longer articulate his feelings will manifest his frustration by his use of his arms and hands. When we are powerless, we indicate our bewilderment by an expression on our faces or by the collapse of our bodies. A father at the side of his dying son may grip the bars of the bed tightly until his fingers show the pressure and tension of his silent agony. We may show joy beyond words by running or dancing, by laughter, or by throwing a stone across the water, a flower into the air, confetti at a wedding. We greet a friend with a handshake that conveys our need for him, our warmth in his presence. We bring guests into our homes by lighting the lights, burning candles, arranging flowers, igniting the fireplace. These are symbols and signs of caring, speaking without words. A parent may hold a child's hand and say nothing; a lover may hold another in his arms and speak no words; a bereaved survivor may lay her head on the shoulder of a friend.

Life is a series of words and symbols, each conveying the mystery of presence. We remember the words and treasure the gifts of those we love. A wed-

ding ring, a birthday present, a keepsake from a deceased brother, the last letter of a soldier-husband may become vital links in our memory of another and in the love we have for his presence.

Worship is, furthermore, a dialogue with one another concerning life and its meaning, death and its nearness, love and its necessity, hope and its grace. It is a conversation with God, of course, but also an act of communion with ourselves. It engages us, when it is genuine, on a level so profound that words fail and signs and symbols are required. And so we praise and petition, remember and regret with our hands and our gifts, our bread and wine, with candles and new fire, lights and embraces, oil and incense, water and salt. We speak of our poverty and our sins, of sorrow and longing, of the losses we sustained, the people we miss, the God we adore.

In his long history, man has developed some words that seemed so apt that he preserved them as traditional prayers, some symbols that said so much that he used them as ritual actions. As each of us grows into maturity, he often remembers the way he was taught to encounter God. We turn to God with our childhood trust, through the turbulence of death or the joy of a wedding, in the birth of children or the confusion of guilt. We repeat the words and the signs that seemed always to reach God and console us. It is no wonder that we are reluctant to discard the words and symbols of traditional worship too easily. They bear something of our own personal history and emotions in their structure.

And yet some change must occur. The words of another era may not express the needs we suffer. The symbols of a former age may not bring us sufficient

life. The memories of childhood may not sustain us in the pain and joy of adulthood.

Each child must learn his own way of speaking a common language. He must speak with his own voice and speech pattern, his own idioms and metaphors. A child who repeats only what his parents say never learns to talk. He becomes a machine that records rather than a person who uses a language. A child must also learn what gifts he wishes to give his mother. The worth of the gift is measured by his choosing it for her rather than by its intrinsic value. He must master the signs of love he wishes to offer his father, the means by which he lets his infant brothers and sisters know of his joy in their birth. He must form a language to suit his identity and become a symbol-maker with the mystery of his own being.

There is a danger in this process. Sometimes we become so content with what we have accomplished by our expressions of self that we tire of finding new ways to declare the changing character of our love and identity. Worship must confess not only the guilt of our ancestors but the sins we wish we had never experienced. It must communicate not only the needs our forefathers felt at the Red Sea but the holocaust and chaos of nuclear weapons, existential alienation, and our own impending death.

Worship changes its words and symbols from time to time. It must do this because life is different when each of us is born. The difference is not so radical that there are no connections with life as it was before our birth. Yet the difference is real enough to require a new name, to account for a new existence, to allow a new personal history to develop in its own way. As ages succeed one another, worship must

note the new names and the new needs. It does this by allowing words and symbols to express not only the way we were but the way we are.

3
RITUAL

Ritual is not spontaneous. A word or a gesture may be spontaneous but ritual is a careful organization of the rites of worship for the sake of the community. A ritual, therefore, is planned. It is not an isolated action.

We have been discussing worship as the expression of profound human needs. Worship is involved with the mystery of presence and with the words and gestures by which we identify ourselves and our experiences. Ritual is part of this process and, therefore, a response to human need.

We organize a birthday party, Thanksgiving, weddings, funerals, homecomings, farewell celebrations. We do this because there are times in life when that which we are about to do is especially significant. In these instances, we plan so that the experience of joy or sorrow may be conveyed unmistakably. We structure the event so that as many as possible may share in the activity and perform specific roles. We parcel out parts, volunteer our services to perform a task, even work out a schedule according to which a speech is made, a gift given, a song sung, a dinner served, music played, a final embrace exchanged, or a first kiss shared. The culture in which one lives determines the tradition or

19

procedure to be followed on these occasions. We find ourselves expecting a cake at a birthday, turkey at Thanksgiving, a tree at Christmas, colored eggs at Easter, lamb at Passover, flowers at a wedding, noise-makers at New Year's.

Our lives are linked by ritual celebrations. If we inherit a tradition and follow a format for less-decisive events, we should not be surprised if there are patterns and procedures expected by a community for its worship. Too much is at stake in worship for its ritual to be left to chance. The structure of worship is not meant to confine freedom but to allow greater meaning. If we do not leave to whim the ar-rangements of a birthday party, it would be foolish to permit worship to occur in a haphazard fashion. We plan because we believe in the worth of that which we are about to do. If, however, we plan too carefully, spontaneity is lost and the plan becomes an end in itself. There is wisdom in learning how to plan flexibly so that individual expression may be en-couraged.

Liturgy is a response to presence. It is a recog-nition prompted by familiar words and conventional symbols arranged in a ritual. Its beauty derives from the fact people become something they do not easily express in their daily lives. They speak of the ul-timate values that bring them through crisis, of the final meaning that gives purpose to the less signifi-cant events. There are those who do not celebrate lit-urgy on this level, but they are always those who come to liturgy for the wrong reasons or who come for the right reasons but discover a liturgy that is dead, inert, and faithless.

Although liturgy uses ritual, it is celebrated

from the substance of human hearts. When the
human heart fails, liturgy suffers. Worship has no
bread but the human heart, nothing to celebrate if
not life itself. Sometimes, however, the problem is
not the human heart of the worshiper but the heart
of the Church or the heart of the celebrant that is
deficient. There may be times in the Church's official life when the liturgy is not attuned as it ought
to be to the needs of people. There are occasions
when the celebrant of a liturgy may have lost his capacity to evoke and express the life of those around
him.

Liturgy, like life, is never problem-free. There is
always a task to be undertaken, a creative path to be
followed, an obstacle to be avoided. Liturgy begins
with care for people and, especially, with a care for
the unspoken dimensions of their lives. It seeks us
out where no one else has ventured, asks questions
no other thought of posing. To deal with liturgy effectively, we must be involved with life and people.

Ritual is an ensemble of words and symbols.
Words are more direct than symbols or ritual, as we
know. In fact, we become impatient when people do
not say clearly what they mean. We know words do
not say it all but we expect them to explain a great
deal. A symbol is, of course, more oblique. It expresses many things simultaneously and requires
words to clarify its intent. A lighted candle is an
enigma unless someone assigns it a meaning verbal-
ly. A symbol employed in the wrong context often
appears silly. Unless words declare its function, the
symbol may seem pretentious, threatening, superflu-
ous, disjointed. We may ridicule, dismiss, or reject
the symbol. Yet a symbol has more potential than

words to become a haunting reality. We might reflect often on the meaning of a gesture or symbol. We perceive something important even if we cannot grasp the precise point. A symbol engages people on a level of seriousness. Because of this, symbols cannot be used in as many different ways as words. Candles used at a burial are not reused for a birthday.

Ritual is even more expansive. It is organized to express and satisfy divergent needs. The essence of its direction is God and a human relationship with him. There are times, of course, when the meaning of the ritual is quite specific. A wedding or a funeral would be examples of this. Religion, however, chooses a central ritualistic action that allows varied responses. The Jewish Seder or the Christian Eucharist would be examples of this.

The most immediate intent of a ritual is the absorption of the person into a fuller life. Triviality is offensive in ritual. Losing oneself in the ritual is most important. When we observe cultures, primitive by Western standards, conduct ritual, we notice how lost its participants become in the chant or the dance. Ecstasy, which literally means to lose oneself, to go out of self, and trance, which means to pass beyond self into something else, often accompany meaningful ritual. One is expected to lose contact with the ordinary and to enter into a state or event, a memory or a hope that captivates and controls.

Ritual is the least controllable, the least rational of religious experiences. It generates a force that magnetizes and frees us. If ritual is reduced to an obligation we must fulfill, we gain little from it. We become involved in a conscious doing of something

for our own sake rather than liberation into a new life. One is not obliged to live; he chooses to do so freely.

If ritual, furthermore, remains something we behold from a distance, it becomes empty. It is comparable to observing life without sensing its force. The emotions of others appear foolish unless we have experienced them personally. We can comprehend the thought processes of those who do not think as we do. But we cannot deal with emotions we have never encountered. Ritual, likewise, is pointless to those who do not participate. Liturgy is tedious when we deal with it coldly, abstractly, merely out of obedience.

Western culture tends to undervalue the emotional expressions that accompany the ritual of other religions. Sometimes these religious acts reach a point of destructive frenzy rather than ecstasy or trance. When this occurs, the shedding of blood or other violent behavior may ensue. Western culture may temper this excess by its emphasis on the worth of the person or by its acceptance of a God who is Father rather than demon, monster, or evil force. Frenzy, however, may be an exaggerated expression of something deficient in Western life. The stress in other cultures on community rather than the individual, on inherited ritual rather than relevant action, on emotion rather than reason, submission in place of volitional control may provide the balance we require for a more effective liturgy.

When religion is properly appreciated, we cannot be adequately human without it. The surrender of all religious values diminishes the person. We have considered thus far the origins of worship in

reverence for the mystery of presence, a presence we encounter in solemn words and sacred symbols. Creative ritual becomes a healing influence when it unites us by bonds that are nonverbal and nonpragmatic, bonds neglected by secular life but forged in religious experience.

An awareness of what we attempt in worship convinces us of its imperatives. Worship becomes obligatory not because we are compelled but because life is irresistible. There is severity as well as serenity in worship as in life. Sacrifice becomes necessary in intense ritual experience. This is not due only to the solemnity of sacrifice that finds an apt place in the solemn enactment of ritual. Nor is it due only to the fact that the God we worship and love is a God to whom we wish to offer ourselves. Ritual creates an environment in which sacrifice makes sense. As ritual draws us out of our self-centeredness, it fills us with the desire for the death of our lesser life for the greater reality we perceive in our ecstasy. Ritual makes us sensitive to the presence of others by the surrender of self-preoccupation.

We do not sacrifice for another because we think it is a good idea or because we are commanded to do so. We sacrifice for another when we participate in his life and when we are eager to do for another that which neither reason requires nor obligation demands. We sacrifice creatively, religiously, poetically when we understand that the sacrifice of self is worthy. We give ourselves away not in rejection but as an invitation to another to make us a gift of his presence. Sacrifice is an encounter with love. Its intent is life. Ritual is the concrete offer of our lives symbolizing a love we cannot forego.

Many have deplored the lack of ritual in modern life. This deficiency may have more to do with our ingrained selfishness than we suspect. Jesus celebrates the ritual of the Passover meaningfully on the night before he dies because he links it with the sacrifice of the cross and with the departure of himself for the gift of the Spirit.

4

COMMUNITY

Community is the way life is meant to happen. It represents more than an association with those who share life with us in the present. It reaches beyond the barrier of death to embrace those who lived before us; it ventures to the horizon of the future where our lives influence those who live after us. We know that human life occurs in a community. We have sensed the need to encounter our brothers and sisters who make up the present human family. In this chapter, we shall consider community in different contexts.

To begin with, we might clarify what we mean by "tradition." Tradition is not, as some suppose, the way we have always done things. Something is not important merely because it is old. People are basically sensible. They would not have preserved tradition over the years unless there were sound reasons. There are two ways of looking at "tradition." One of these involves the perpetuation of habitual customs, customs people are reluctant to change because they have become used to them or because a particular vested interest is threatened. These customs do not approach tradition on the level we wish to consider. Such customs are relatively trivial; they are the substance of nostalgia, the object of what we

call "old-fashioned" ways. These customs ought to cede to progress; they are never as vital to people as they seem; most often they continue because no one has thought to question them.

Tradition, in the larger sense, is another matter. It is the medium through which life is transferred from one generation to another. In his play *The Skin of Our Teeth*, Thornton Wilder refers to books and the wisdom in them as indispensable to human survival. We do not wish to disregard the importance of words as man's way of keeping himself alive. Before writing, oral tradition or storytelling transmitted truth and wisdom. Language, spoken or written, is a uniquely human mode of life. Tradition, however, is enacted nonverbally. It changes less quickly than language. It is the most decisive element by which we hand down the unspoken and unspeakable realities of life. Tradition is desperately clung to because its passing represents the death of life. Without tradition, we become strangers to those who lived before us and whose lives influenced tradition; we deprive ourselves of a life in the future contained in the tradition we hand over to the next generation.

In order to inherit tradition, we must live in a community. Communities preserve tradition because they preserve life. Until a community has a tradition to impart, it is not a community but merely a society or an institute or an assembly. A community, furthermore, is never as alive as when its members celebrate tradition. A family is intensely alive when it celebrates a birthday or a wedding, Thanksgiving or Christmas, Passover or Easter. It is cohesive, aware of the bonds that hold it together when it enacts the tradition of a funeral or the means by which it re-

members those who are no longer living. The Church is most itself when it celebrates the Eucharist and renews the tradition of the Last Supper. The Jewish community identifies itself by the annual experience of Passover.

Tradition reminds us and declares to others the fact that we did not originate recently. We are here because a history of life preceded us. We were not born yesterday or the day before but in a past when we were given no name and when no date for our birth could be determined. We were alive in the caves and the forests, sons and daughters of those who painted prehistoric animals and symbols, brothers and sisters of families who wandered the deserts, ascended the mountains, set sail on the perilous seas. The record of our birth as a race is traced in our veins, embedded in our genetic structure, etched in our memories. Our eyes have beheld more than we now see. On occasion, we wonder whether we have lived before, citizens of a land we never visited, strangely familiar with faces we should have known but cannot recall. There is a continuity to our race, a kinship in our family. We do not know all the connections, remember all the names, recall the various greetings or gestures by which brotherhood is celebrated. But we know, in our bones and flesh, in our blood and tears, in our wonder and sadness that the history of who we were and are has not been made complete by words or reasons.

Contemporary man has been bewildered by what to make of the past. He loses his way with the present when he neglects tradition. Life becomes flat, one-dimensional; the crises we encounter lack perspective; an awareness of all the human family

has survived is obscured and we become anxious concerning the future; our identity is subjected to serious doubt; we become victims of the present, paralyzed by its problems, perplexed by its pressures. In a family, grandparents assure us by their presence that life is not unbearably harsh and that the suffering of our present dilemmas are less severe than they appear. In the Church, we are reminded that Jesus conquered death itself and that the Word of the Lord, a Word of love and hope, cannot be abolished.

The Eucharist is the central tradition of the Christian community. Jesus could not communicate all he wished to reveal on the night before his death. He broke bread and shared wine, asking us to remember. This breaking of the bread, endlessly renewed, would reveal to believers truths about life and faith that none of us is wise enough to formulate. We go back in memory to that night repeatedly and gain hope from this past event. We evoke the fear and the love of Jesus, the candlelight and the washings, the communion and embraces of that night that simultaneously initiated and tested our devotion. The tradition is simple, spare, sad, serene. The words of Jesus and about Jesus would lose their force if we did not break bread in silence and preserve the tradition in love.

The tradition we re-enact in our liturgy is the most dramatic means by which we impart Christ and impart ourselves to one another. No tradition can be vital, however, unless sacrifice and gift-giving attend it. When we give our faith to one another in the breaking of the bread, we bring tradition to life. We hand over to a new generation not only Jesus but

also ourselves. This gift is given in the hope that the future will not refuse our faith or allow Jesus to perish. The forms by which the tradition is imparted become important because they are channels of life, sacraments and structures that bear the grace of our presence and the memory of our love.

It is no wonder, then, that religion changes liturgy reluctantly. A violent reform might estrange us from tradition, the past, and the Spirit of Jesus. The fiercest contestations among Christians of the past and present have been waged over seemingly trivial but potentially significant questions. Christians have divided over the date of Easter, the age of baptism, the designation of celebrants of the Eucharist, the meaning of the breaking of the bread, the number of witnesses at a wedding or godparents at a christening, the manner in which the dead are burned or buried. Admittedly, many of these matters were subterfuges for cynical attempts to wield power or blinders by which the narrow-minded fought to retain their myopia. Nonetheless, emotions sometimes became intense because the credibility of the past and the reliability of the present were the real issues debated beneath the surface.

Tradition reveals to us, furthermore, the nature of human life. Man is a memory-making, memory-keeping creature. His memories do not merely recall the past; they bring the life of the past into the present and they form the substance of hope for the future. A future with no past is absurd and impossible. Memory-making is most dramatic in the formulation of myth and the creation of tradition.

It all fits together. We learn this or we learn little about life. Life is a series of connections. When

we perceive the connections that bind us to the past and the future, to Christ and to one another, to the strangers on the road and the friends in our home, when we connect water with wine, bread with Jesus, faith with doubt, tradition with presence, we are healed and become whole.

It is a truism to declare that we need one another to survive. Liturgy reminds us of this fact but it also underscores a factor easily neglected by contemporary man. It tells us we need the dead as well as the living for our survival; it assures us the future requires our life and death for its accomplishment. Liturgy, therefore, creates the most expansive and extensive community imaginable. It invites into our assembly the Father we have not seen, the Jesus who lived before our birth, the Spirit who makes us children, the dead who once gave us life, the unborn we are obliged to create, the living we have alienated, the family we befriend, even the betrayer, the enemy who receives our love in the very act by which he denies us further life.

The liturgy is a community-forming experience. It makes a community not of convenience or commerce, not of comfort or accommodation but a community of sacrifice and the cross, of nourishment and rebirth, of Pentecostal fires and apocalyptic expectations. The community of faith celebrates the agony of Jesus and the breaking of his heart, the death of the apostles and the blood of the martyrs. But it also announces the future and reveals the Easter life of Christ; it preserves the wine of final victory and calls attention to the coronation of the saints and the glorification of the innocent. No one must be neglected. No one is left out of the circle. If one of

us who wishes to be present is missed, the family is incomplete and the circle broken. If one name is forgotten, one life extinguished, one place at the table of life left empty, it would not be heaven. The liturgy of heaven is a community of love begun in the ancient tradition of Eden and celebrated fully as the earth passes into the life of God.

5
FAITH

Faith is not an ethereal phenomenon. It occurs concretely through persons whose names we know, in events we narrate, and in experiences we can describe. Faith leads us back to people, from whose lives faith originates. No person believes alone. He measures his faith by what others have seen and integrates it in the context of other lives. He believes for the sake of life if he believes at all. Life is not an ethereal experience. It too lives by names and places, by events and familiar faces, by recognizable rituals and measurable realities.

Worship plays a twofold role in its relationship with faith. It is the end result of that which faith seeks; it is sometimes the means by which we begin to consider faith as a commitment we wish to make. Liturgy, therefore, ought to be a careful endeavor. Celebrated properly, it is a singular grace for the person who hoped for a form faith might take. An effective liturgy is a revelation for those who see in it a concrete manifestation of the faith they require. It is not words or symbols or ritual but the people who worship who ultimately convince us of faith's credibility. Encounter with people in a liturgical context gives us a different view of human life. It becomes an epiphany of the faith obscured in more secular

meetings, a faith whose force even believers themselves underestimate until the liturgy brings to con-
sciousness the full reality of faith's power.

Liturgy is linked to the Church by faith. By its
very existence the Church implicitly promises to become a liturgical community, a community in which
faith will be celebrated as a central event. The
Church proclaims Christ as a universal invitation for
believers to form a community. Through its liturgy,
the Church offers a home to those who have no abiding city, those who cannot put their trust in kings or
princes, those who find it wasteful to fill their barns
with grain and profit. In a sense, the Church is an
assembly of the desperate. It offers hope for people
who have no final hope, no further faith than that
which Christ represents. Faith is a desperate endeav-
or, not because it lacks serenity or sense nor because
it attracts those who evade responsibility. It is for
the disinherited, not the delinquent. It is not for
those who seek no more but for those who have not
yet found their way. It is desperate; it believes that if
Christ is not true, there is nowhere else to go. It
senses that without Christ the lights of the universe
will one day be dimmed and a realm of unending
night will follow.

Faith calls us out of this darkness. Faith is the
fire by which Christ is illumined in the world. Faith
is worship's first moment, and liturgy is faith's ritual
form.

There is a venerable phrase that retains its vital-
ity, "*lex orandi, lex credendi.*" It means that one
knows his faith by how he prays. If a person accepts
God as a terrifying reality, he will pray constantly to
be delivered, ask endlessly for mercy, make guilt and

forgiveness the center of his every prayer. In this case, faith is fear and God a frightening force. If a person believes that God should make life go his own way, he will pray for favors. His faith will depend upon the number of petitions God grants. God will be addressed as a cosmic wonder-worker and a personal patron. If a person relates to God as a Father, he will pray in gratitude, serenely, contemplatively. He will marvel not at the possibility God may do more but at the fact God has already exceeded that which we deserve. On an even more remarkable level, there are those whose faith in God is not motivated by forgiveness, petition, or even gratitude. The highest prayer is commensurate with the bravest faith. Some rejoice merely because God exists. This is the final achievement in any relationship, human or divine. It is joy emerging from the nearness of those one will not forfeit. It is faithfulness deriving not from what God or another does but from who they are. As we believe, so we pray. Prayer reveals both God and the character of our own faith.

The same role we have shown to be operative for individuals remains valid for communities. The Church prays out its faith in worship. It creates a liturgical sign so that its faith might have a discernible form. It sings and proclaims, dances and dramatizes its belief so that the world may behold the grandeur and pain that is faith.

We might wonder, however, why liturgy would be important for those whose faith is both personal and secure. This question has been raised often by contemporary man. Such a question would have little meaning for people many centuries ago. Faith, in the past, had been so public a matter, worship so

social a form that one would seldom question its necessity for himself or his obligation to perform accustomed rituals. The rites of initiation into life or into the tribe included the names of the gods, the history of their deeds, the imperatives they imposed. One expressed, for example, his Jewishness by the performance of religious as well as social actions. Today, we may be troubled by people who believe by convention rather than from faith. We discourage people from using worship merely for its societal or commercial advantages.

It is worth recalling, nonetheless, that conventions were once the essence of religious rites. People worshiped because society was considered a sacred community; acceptance into the social order was a liturgical experience. This is not true today, at least in the same way as before. Society is now viewed as an exclusively secular task. We are not suggesting that there were not insecure people in the past nor that such a fusion of convention and faith, of society and religion was a preferable alternative. We are reminding ourselves that religion became conventional because conventions were once religious actions. Obedience to elders or parents was considered docility to God; tribal traditions were a religious heritage; conventions contained revelations and gave one a sense of his relationship with God; grace had more to do with the welfare of the tribe, its crops or hunt, its wars or health, than with personal advantages. The destiny of the community rather than the survival of the individual was paramount. When an individual was troubled in heart, tormented by pain, afflicted in ways he could not comprehend, he went to his tribe for healing. Witchcraft or incantation

were valued not because of their intrinsic medicinal virtues but because they were sanctioned by the tribe's history. It was not one's own resources that made the difference but the strength and grace of the community. In such a context, one would never consider his personal faith so secure that public worship could be discarded.

Liturgical history is filled with the energy of human love and hope. It is a record of pain and fear, a record we could not lose without surrendering a vital element in man's identity. Christianity is most effective when its worship marks not an interruption but a liturgical continuity with pre-Christian and non-Christian celebration.

On the night when Jesus broke bread and asked to be loved, the upper room was illuminated, in a sense, by the fires that flickered in the caves as primitive man painted religious symbols, and by the light against the sky as crops or animals were burned in sacrifice on the plains of history. Jesus reached by his action the stirrings of the human heart that has always hoped for God and wept for relief in his discovery. The wine Jesus drank was a communion with his own Jewish tradition, a way by which he declared himself a member of the tribe, one who loved its community and needed its people. The wine of that evening was a symbol of all the libations men offered their gods, of all the oil and honey men poured into the earth to tell God they wished to live for more than their own advantage.

It is faith that gathers together the loose threads of history, the seemingly disconnected experiences by which men love and wonder. When reason is applied too sharply to the process, the subtle interconnec-

tions are unraveled and history appears haphazard. Evolution is dangerous when it leads us to believe in absolute progress or to suppose that we build on the death of the past or make the future by disrupting all that is venerable in human history.

The last place many of our contemporaries would look for the answer to modern problems is worship. Yet the secret and mystery by which man has traced his name on the heavens with his arms and hands, the grandeur or grief that led him to shout for God in the wilderness, the heavy but unbroken spirit that caused him to bury his friends in the darkness with the tools they would require for another life, these profoundly moving moments of human history must be dealt with by modern man if he would not lose his humanness.

Faith and the form it takes in worship allows us to view our lives in perspective and proportion. This is what prayer is all about, the achievement of balance by acknowledging neglected elements in the equation of life. If men would survive and persevere, they must refuse to be anxious and too much troubled by the crises through which history always passes. Worship is often the searching out of resources in life more expansive than the pain or anguish of the present moment. Worship makes us serene not only because we touch God in the darkness but because we enter into communion with our brothers and sisters of the past who overcame the same crises that now disturb us. Worship lends perspective to history not as historians might, by analysis and reason, by research or chronology, but as people have done before history, by an intuitive acceptance of the wholeness of the universe and the

permanence of time. The morning after a night of crushing grief bears the dawn and wakens us to life; the early sunlight makes fire unnecessary and turns the ashes of the evening grey against a new beginning. It is wisdom to realize that the universe is colored with life everytime we despair of it.

Faith and worship were intended as exciting realities. They became dull when man separated himself from the larger community of life and tried to deal with reality only in terms of his subjective responses. We asked earlier why one would require worship if his faith were both personal and secure. Worship is needed because such an individual faith, though valid, is incomplete. Because it is incomplete, it is easily threatened by crisis; its fragility is often shattered by existential loneliness or the subjective fears that lead to despair. The meaninglessness of modern life is often the result of losing the power of the community. If man has no community to heal him, he wanders through life wounded, sensitive, forever bleeding on the cross, unable to discover God or his friends.

Worship is important because it takes us out of ourselves, sometimes into the past, sometimes into a wider present, sometimes into the future. We distinguished earlier the difference between convention and faith. The contribution of our age lies in its demand for authenticity and sincerity from the believer. It invites consideration not only of the social consequences of faith but of the personal character of belief. It seeks us out as persons rather than as a tribe and it holds worthwhile the individual destiny of each life. To this extent, the nontribal emphasis of the modern age is healthy. It is necessary, however,

to discover the link between convention and faith so that one can overcome the false distinction between the secular and the sacred.

The modern age has enabled us to realize that many realities once assigned directly to God are the result of natural forces. We have yet to appreciate, however, the sacredness of those natural forces that eventually lead to the creation of human life. The modern age has shown how the political realities, the pragmatic necessities, and economic pressures of society are not God's work but our own. We have yet to understand, however, the sacredness or the origins of that drive which leads men into community or the fullness of that reality we call society as it teaches us conventions and liturgy, language and love, crafts for survival and rituals for communication.

When a Christian comes to the Eucharist, he must come with memories from the past. He is invited to recall Jesus and the crisis of his life as he broke bread in the brokenness of his heart. He is asked to celebrate a death that was no death because Jesus found a place to put his excruciating defeat. Jesus set his dying into his Father's hands and into the community's life. Worship is a relief from the preoccupations of the present, a healing with memory and hope. Faith is the air the liturgy breathes; without it, worship becomes rigid, sterile, and dies; with faith, worship is ignited by the Spirit of Jesus and our empty hearts are filled with the fire of life and the light of love.

6
JESUS

In the first chapter, we discussed the sense of presence that is at the heart of worship. In the succeeding chapter, we dealt with realities that were applicable to other religions as much as to Christianity. We made an effort to understand how words and symbols form a ritual and develop a community. All religions verbalize, symbolize, ritualize their faith; all of them form a community. In this sense, Christianity is one of the world's many religions. In the final four chapters of this book, we shall deal with Christianity more exclusively. We shall indicate, of course, that Christian realities are present in other religions but our main interest will be devoted to a consideration of how and why Christians worship.

The Scriptures relate that awesome moment when God tells his name to his people. God becomes not only a presence they sense but a name they call. To give someone a name or to tell another one's name is a significant action. Only those who assume care for another and accept responsibility for him are entitled to give him a name. Even children perceive this. They know if they name a pet they must care for it. Giving a name creates a bond of affection. They are aware that their parents and not

43

themselves will name a new brother or sister. In naming another, we initiate his process of identity. Names unite us to those we love. Even the way we say the names of others is a measure of how we value them. In pain or joy, in loneliness or love, the name of another has a power all its own. One of the most bitter of life's experiences occurs when we call those we love and they do not respond because of disability or unwillingness. Almost the first interest in the birth of a child is his name; a person's name is often the last word breathed into his ear. We do this because we know one will hear his name even if he can hear nothing else.

Anonymity, having no name, has a relationship with nonexistence. We are completely lost when we confuse our way home and forget our name. We are delighted when those we value remember our names after long absences or infrequent meetings. "He did not even know my name" is a complaint that reverberates with alienation and disappointment.

When Pope John XXIII gave himself a new name for visiting rabbis ("I am Joseph, your brother"), they understood that he intended to become someone else for them and signified this by using a different name.

We are reluctant to tell others our name until we have established a relationship with them. In the ancient world, people were even more hesitant. They would sometimes spend days with another before declaring their name. When they did, their hosts understood that their guests trusted them. Even today we answer strangers who ask us for incidental information more readily than those who question us for our name.

The name of the presence we seek in worship indicates our relationship with him. In some religions, the presence has no name so that aloofness, sometimes terror, characterizes the experience with God. In those religions where God is named, love follows more easily. The God of the Scriptures is not a God of incidental information but a God for relationship. In Jewish religion, there is only one God and he entrusts his name to his people. He asks his people to name the animals and to care for one another. He promises not to leave his people orphans or nameless. Between God and man there is to be no anonymity.

Christians have called Jesus God's Son; they encounter God through the name of Christ. In Jesus, Christians affirm that God has a name but also a human heart and a personal history. The New Testament account of the conception of Jesus excludes the parents from naming the child. The name is given from heaven as a sign that God has a special care and a singular responsibility for this life.

In Jesus, Christians confess God's name. Christianity does not recognize many gods, or accept a different god for each culture. There is only one God, one human family, one history for all. Christianity preaches that Jesus is the proper name for the God all men seek under other names.

How can we make this claim and yet remain sensitive to the fact that other cultures have found God and that we do not know all there is to know about God? The most fruitful of man's collaborative efforts will be realized when the religions and cultures of the world dialogue about the nature of the presence and the name of the Person who has given

life to all. Many of our contemporaries are impressed by the efforts we are making to achieve economic and political alliances in the world. These appear more important than they are. Economic alliances are less important than the human values, the philosophical presuppositions, the religious affirmations that operate in human life even if not explicitly stated. If men appreciated life properly, there would be food and fuel, medical care and adequate homes for all our brothers and sisters. The world does not value life adequately. And so we go our way, creating systems that mask greed or aggressiveness, pride or power. One day we shall admit the fact that men are not saved even by bread but by respect for the life that flows in their veins and breathes in their flesh.

Political alliances, moreover, are often premised on principles disguised by diplomatic language. Unfortunately, many fundamentalistic preachers have presented religious values as the answer to human problems so simplistically that they have made a religious reform of the world sound inane, absurd, nonsensical. Yet the truth persists even though its presentation is deformed. This problem is worthy of fuller elaboration.

Two of the most critical and haunting questions that ring through the Gospel are these: "I know what others have said of me, but who do you say I am?" and "Who is my neighbor, the brother I must keep, the sister I must not deny?" These questions emerge at different moments in the Gospel message but they belong together. The answer to one of these questions requires careful attention to the other.

Who do you say I am? The ancient question,

raised in primeval forests and nameless deserts. The ancient question, "Who am I?" Men have heard it echoed on the ageless seas and in the hidden caves where once we lived. We have gone into isolation, into eremetical life, gathered in monasteries and churches, raised cathedrals, built shrines on the mountains as a way of learning the name or beholding the face of God. One day, a young Jewish man, Nazareth-bred, Bethlehem-born, a man who healed by the disturbance he caused, asked his disciples on the plains of a desolate city, "Who am I?"

The disciples heard in his voice, read in his eyes, the old, the very old question. This is the voice that called their fathers out of Egypt and inspired them to build the sacred city of Jerusalem on a mountain of Israel. Moses saw those eyes in the burning fire that did not destroy and in the clouds of Sinai where lightning made the law. Abraham felt the power of that question when, bewildered, he was ready to slay his son. Lord, who are you? What is your name? What do you expect from us?

Who do you say I am? The name, the name. What is the name of this man, this God, this Savior, this Messiah whose question will not leave us. "I am Who am" God once declared in the desert. But this Jesus has a history, a mother and a father, a native city, a Galilean dialect, a certain age, a distinctive manner, a face we recognize in the darkness of the Garden or the noon brightness of Calvary. We cannot call him "I am Who am" because we know so much about him. Jesus is his name, the Christ not only for this band of believers but Jesus in the most universal terms imaginable.

Jesus is the "I am Who am" of the distant ages.

He is God's Son and the Spirit is in him; he is our brother and the Shepherd of all who learn love. We do not know all there is to know of him. But we know his name. A name is the beginning of a relationship and the first sign of friendship. To learn more of him, we must learn more of one another. God is not discovered until every brother and sister is named and loved. It is a long process. This is why the identity of Jesus cannot be limited to Christians. In the Stone Age, men sensed the presence and encountered God in ways we do not. He became the God they needed. In their tools and symbols, in their painted messages and burial customs, they revealed the Jesus they knew without knowing his name. In the silence of Hindu contemplation, no names are spoken but the presence and identity of Jesus exists for those who hear without words or spoken language. In the nonviolence of Buddhism, the violence by which Jesus suffered is perceived in a manner Christians cannot grasp. When we have absorbed the nonviolence of Buddhism, we shall know of Easter in a new way. Without Judaism, there is no Jesus, no name, no birth for God, no mother, disciple, or Eucharist.

"Who do you say I am?" To answer this question without asking "Who is my brother, where is my sister?" is to be destined to constant error. And so we seek, not only the name by which God is to be called but the bonds that bind us to those we thought belonged to us in no way, those of another race, a different tribe, an alien family. Names, names. We need all the names before we can utter God's name properly. Faces, in all their forms, we must see all the faces before the eyes of God will let us rest and

accept our answer to his persistent question, "Who do you say I am?"

One of the most crucial lessons Jesus teaches is the necessity to feel secure with strangers. A stranger is someone who sees something in life we cannot live with comfortably. There is something in his eyes, the manner of his speech, the motives that quicken his heart, the things he hears that we do not recognize. The stranger is the one who allows us to live on another level, to learn a new name in our answer to the question "Who do you say I am?" The mystery of the Christ lies hidden in the eyes of countless strangers not insofar as they are strangers but because we require their alternative visions of life so that Jesus may be whole. We must take the stranger home, make room in the inn, bind up the wounds of an alien Samaritan or a prodigal son so that we might worship effectively.

And so, when Christians declare Jesus the center, they do not exclude other religions but invite them into the circle. For the circle has no center without them. If it be true, as Christians maintain, that Jesus is indispensable, they do not value less the spiritual riches of other religions. Rather, they search for those non-Christians who can make Christ real in a way Christians cannot. They do not intend, if they be genuine in their Christianity, dominion, superiority, or self-vindication. A discontent with their fellow believers sends them into the strangeness of other religions so that they may find Christ. This discontent does not mean that Christians fail especially, but it does mean that we are all deficient until there are no further strangers.

Jesus is the presence men have yearned to call

and waited to hear. He appears among us as the poor man, the stranger, because he knows that the poor and the strangers are those least likely to be invited into the circle. We have made more room than necessary for the wealthy and the powerful, those whose names we know and whose faces chance has allowed us to recognize. But God is the God of poverty and strangeness, the Savior who redeems us from the familiar. He wanders into the wilderness to make a beginning where men thought no new life was possible. Jesus, the Christ, is the answer Christians give when asked, "But who do you say I am?" The liturgy is the celebration of that discovery, the repetition of that name, the hope that the faithful presence of Jesus will abide with us, father us into new life, brother us into a new community, love us so invincibly that we shall be forced to love one another.

It has been an arduous journey, through history, sometimes namelessly, to Christ. And the journey continues. But now we know the name and see the road. The name is Jesus and the road by which we journey is the love we bear one another. So many times the road was confused, the presence fleeting. We got the name wrong so often, sacrificed things that should not have been forsaken. But now we know. The sacrifice required is the sacrifice of our strangeness to one another. As this is burnt away, God emerges from the burning bush or the flaming mountain of his love. And he sets us on fire with love for one another, a fire that burns the Spirit of Jesus into the hearts of all of us who once thought we had different roads to travel or diverse gods to worship. It has been a long journey, indeed, and we almost

lost the direction. For God came in poverty and strangeness and only a few stopped to ask his name and invite him into the circle. They went out of their way to inquire and they did this for the sake of all. God, surprisingly, was not on the road but on the side, pleading in his blindness and poverty for someone to receive him. And to those who received him, he entrusted the mystery of his name and offered them everlasting life.

7
SACRAMENTS

A sacrament is a sign that the presence we have sought is nearby and favorable. It is a symbol so rich that it is accompanied by words, music, and dance. A symbol is effective as long as its meaning is relatively clear. It is true, of course, that the symbol signifies a great mystery. One, after all, does not create a symbol for trivial events. But the symbol should be understandable so that what is said about the mystery may be well said. There is always a danger that the symbol might be used to express only the subjective world of the symbol-maker. For this reason, religious communities seek to influence the way symbols are structured. Religious symbols bear the burden of transmitting not only the faith of individuals but the tradition and identity of a community.

When symbols are integrated into a ritual, a community forms. Sacraments are ritualized symbols. Since they seek a relationship between God and man, they are also acts of worship. A sacrament is a Christian evocation of Jesus. We offer our physical lives to God so that we might be washed or anointed, nourished or healed by his life. We require communion with God especially in those experiences that exceed our resources. Birth and sickness, marriage and ministry, absolution and community are so mys-

terious that they prompt us to invite God into the
circle of our lives and to ask that he take us into the
center of his existence. Sacraments offer the gift of
love on higher levels of meaning. We celebrate sacraments so that new forms of life and further oppor-
tunities for love might be given.

Life, in its first innocence and grace, is given in
baptism; the life of age and wisdom is given in con-
firmation; the life of forgiveness overcomes the death
of our guilt and the life of healing prevails over the
pain and brokenness of our sickness; the life of form-
ing life for others in community is granted in ministry and marriage; the life of Jesus as he makes us
disciples for the sake of one another is bestowed in
the breaking of the bread. These forms of life are
forms of love. Birth and growth, forgiveness and
healing, ministry and marriage, discipleship and
community are actions of love. They make no sense
unless they are motivated by love.

Although the alternative may appear inviting,
the religious lives of people would become confused
and chaotic if the community did not influence worship in a responsible manner. Worship is a dialogue
between subjective needs and community require-
ments. We affirm something larger than ourselves in
worship, not only the God who is more than we are
but the community that encounters reality more uni-
versally than we do. A tension ensues as we make
room in the liturgy not only for God but also for
ourselves, not only for the community as such but
also for the persons who compose it. Worship is
most effective when the community, realizing the
diversity of individual gifts, gives guidelines rather
than details, patterns rather than rubrics, and when

persons discipline themselves to this context. This
procedure is not as imperative in instances of personal devotion or private prayer because the entire
tradition of a community is not as formally involved
in these actions. Sacraments, however, are the means
by which Christian faith is passed on from one generation to the next. The manner in which a new generation perceives a venerable faith must be a community concern.

The fuller dimensions of sacramental worship
reveal the tradition of the Church, the identity of
Christ, the character of one's faith. Sacraments not
only invite Christ into the decisive experiences of our
lives; they also alert us to the life of Christ. Baptism
reminds us that Christ intends life as a ministry of
service. Anointing and penance make us aware that
Christ expects human life to resist the tyranny of
pain and the terror of guilt. Marriage and Eucharist
recall Christ's unity with us and the transformation
of creation capable through the power of love. The
light of the sacraments is the strength by which the
Christian community preserves its heritage, main-
tains its life, and consecrates others with grace.

The New Testament speaks of a priesthood of
all believers. We have understood priesthood lately
to refer to sacramental life in a specific manner.
Many identify the priest as the only one able to
preside at the Eucharist or effect the liturgical forgiveness of sins. In other words, a special jurisdiction
or sacramental capacity is deemed the distinguishing
criterion for ordained ministry. Baptism, however,
consecrates every Christian as a priest. This is the
first and richest of the Church's traditions. Indeed,
centuries later, the Reformation led to the division

of Christianity over this very issue. In order to clarify the meaning of sacraments, we might inquire what a priest is. The understanding of ordained ministry is linked with the conception we have of Christ and his Church.

We saw in the last chapter that Christ is a brother, someone whose needs are so great that he remains responsive to the needs of others. He enters our family, marked for death, sacrificial in his life, tragic in his incomprehensible innocence. The disciple of Christ is expected to absorb as much of Christ's identity into his life as his own identity can sustain. He too is a brother or a sister for us and, hence, able to minister to us and grace our lives. Baptism is a brother-making, sister-making sacrament. It is priestly because it is familial, Christic because it creates a service rather than an office or title. A priest is someone who is sensitive to the needs of others with the poverty of his life and the sacrifice of his love. Every Christian becomes a priest, therefore, as he accepts ministry on two levels. He becomes a priest as he allows his heart to be formed by the spirit of Christ and the needs of others. This priesthood is internal, personal, not given by the official Church but imparted through the charism of an individual relationship with Christ. But priesthood in the Christian community requires an additional dimension, namely, a sacramental expression. Baptism summons us out of darkness into the wonderful light of priesthood. It is the consecration of a priest in oil and water, salt and candlelight, name-giving and prayer. Baptism is an action of the Church, a liturgical, official action of worship meant to complement the internal priesthood of one's heart.

Christ establishes a relationship with all who love, irrespective of age or condition, rank or intelligence, preparation or aptitude. He is not incarnate in an office but in the actions of love. The priesthood is a means of imitating Christ in this manner. Without love, priesthood is secular formalism in ecclesiastical legalism. It absorbs the worst of two worlds. With love, priesthood is as universal and invincible as the life of Christ and the Church becomes indestructible through it. As an organized community, the Church must designate its priests explicitly. It does this by Baptism.

Baptism, therefore, is ordination to the substance of priesthood, namely, love and service publicly, officially, liturgically designated as a sacramental reality.

The Church is a community that presents Christ equally to all. It is a vocation universal in its call, sacrificial in its demand that we serve one another. The Church is a community that makes priests of believers and expects ministry from everyone. Christ allows no one a passive role in his community. He could not do otherwise because a community is never content with indifferent or passive persons. Christ and the Church are not the prerogative of the few, the privilege of a particular group, the prisoners of those who restrict them to whom they choose. Christianity is limitless and unpredictable. Anyone may be summoned for priesthood in the Church because everyone is meant for love. The Church ordains to the priesthood even infants whose hearts and gifts, intentions and choices cannot be discerned. But the Church knows already that if these new Christians wish to remain in the community, they must perform a priestly service. This new vocation for the newly

born is symbolized by the new name they are given. The name "Jesus" is spoken in their presence, his cross traced upon their breasts. Newly born, they are already marked for death, tragic in their incomprehensible innocence, sacrificial in the demands of love placed upon them, priestly in their anointing for service, Christic in the Spirit they receive, Catholic because they are meant for all, Christians because they are required to bear light in the darkness. Baptism is a very venerable, very ancient, truly apostolic tradition of the Church.

We have yet to explain, however, how or why it is that some in our community are priests in another way. What tradition or necessity has created an ordained as well as a baptized priesthood? The tradition that provides for this is also very ancient, truly apostolic and necessary. A community lives in different ways and has specialized needs. In a family, a mother has a different vocation from that of her son, a father a distinct identity from that of his daughter, and yet the family belongs indiscriminately to all. When one person in a family is deemed more important than another, the family suffers. Fatherhood or motherhood are gifts to others and never self-gratifying or isolating offices. Differences of roles in the family cannot be denied and should not be denied. The differences are the essence of a valid community as long as the differences are not considered important as ends in themselves. The difference is intended as an effective way of dying to self and as the basis for uniting with others, transforming diversity into communion. Christ, Paul tells us, does not cling to his divinity but, remaining God's Son, nonetheless empties himself, becoming one with us, not so that

he might remain different but so that he might transform us into his life.

Baptism, we have noted, is given in hope. Before one can discern the identity of a Christian, he is assigned a priestly task in the community. The scrutiny is more rigorous in offering the ordained priesthood. This is not because it is a more important office but because its function is so specialized that it requires specific disciplines and gifts. It is less generic than the universal priesthood. Yet even the ordained priesthood must be given in hope. The ordained priest is not really unique because he is designated to celebrate sacraments others may not. If this were the essence of such a vocation, less hope and risk would be involved. The ordained priest is the one whose vocation it is to form a community of Christians and to preside over it by the sacrifice of his love. He is the one who officially calls a community of the baptized into a special relationship with one another. To aid him in this ministry, the Church trains him and seeks to discern the gifts of his heart. It then ordains him in the hope that his service may lead him to cling to his community rather than to his office, and to empty himself so that he might be transformed into the community as its elder brother even as he transforms the community into the life of Christ, who shepherds us all. The priest always celebrates the Eucharist uniquely because his vocation in the community is unique. Although the celebration of this sacrament need not be limited to the ordained ministry, it is fitting that the most important community-forming sacrament be most often celebrated by the one whose essential ministry is the formation of a community of the baptized.

The priesthood emerges from the very life of the community. It is as natural to a community of faith as brotherhood or sonship is natural to a family. Whether this priesthood is baptized or ordained, it belongs to the one community and is utilized in ways people require.

The human family once required Christ for its life. And God sent him to us. The Father offered his Son, baptized in the River Jordan when his ministry needed expression in this manner, ordained on the cross by the bread and wine of his consecration when his ministry required fulfillment in another manner. This Jesus became truly the Christ for us, the anointed one, the limitless and everlasting priest of this community, because his ministry was responsive to the community's universal needs and redemption. No Christian believes Christ has been isolated from us because of his special ministry. Rather, we glory and live, grow and are graced by the very difference and distinction. This is because Jesus used the difference on our behalf and allowed the distinction to become the essence of his communion with us.

When a Christian, baptized into the priesthood of Christ, uses this distinction to assert his supposed superiority over a non-Christian or to develop an aloofness from a supposedly inferior world, he betrays Christ and forfeits the faithfulness of his priesthood. When another Christian, ordained into the priesthood of Christ, uses his ministry to affirm the Church or Christ as his special prerogative and to develop structures for self-gratification, remaining aloof from those supposedly less necessary to Christ or the Church than he is, he dies not to himself but to the life he might have given. He betrays not an of-

fice but the need Christians had for him so that their lives are impoverished rather than enriched because of his ordination.

There are sacraments in this community because Christ was here and remains with us. There are sacraments in this community because life must happen and because Christians are destined to minister life. There are sacraments in this community because the compassion of Christ and the birth of Jesus, the memory of Christ and the growth of Jesus, the priesthood of Christ and the forgiveness of Jesus must be real events for us rather than ephemeral ideas or past occurrences. We require concreteness for life. Sacraments force us out of vagueness and ambiguity into a historical community where love happens inescapably and unavoidably, with all the inevitability of death and all the urgency of life. Sacraments are no more dispensable than water and nourishment; they are as necessary as names and places.

The Christian community, therefore, does not celebrate sacraments as peripheral actions. It lives by sacraments. It believes in sacraments because it believes in life, in the Christ who is present through them, in the community that emerges from them. Sacraments were not required when Christ was here as a sacramental sign, with his own words to offer us and his flesh and blood to touch and heal us. Sacraments will not be necessary when Christ returns. For then, the concrete nearness of Christ will refresh us in innocence and impart to us the oil of gladness in a communion as deep as marriage and as lasting as ministry. Sacraments are not for those who are to be saved. They are for those who know this and who

anticipate that which all our brothers and sisters will one day discover. Sacraments do not save a few but commit those who celebrate them to a universal ministry.

8
SPIRIT

The world needs relief from its material deceptions. This has been a concern of religions from their inception. Hindus so distrust the material world that they counsel flight from it. Buddhists try to interpret matter in a radically spiritual fashion. Judaism has as its first commandment the fact that no god must be placed before the God of Israel. Christianity derives from the Easter witness of an unconquerable Spirit.

The peril of belief in the spirit is the blindness it may cause to the reality of the material world. Christianity has made its own effort to counteract this tendency by its insistence on the Incarnation, the sacramental system, a visible Church, and the resurrection of the dead. The effort is not always successful. The Church sometimes favors a spirituality that leads to personal piety rather than true devotion, one that dismisses real problems with official rhetoric, or offers sacramental solutions when social and ecclesial reform is required. This is unfortunate but not even an institution with Christ as its central concern manages life perfectly. One must remain sensitive to the imperfections without neglecting the terrible need the contemporary world has for a community that criticizes the illusion of material progress. At

times, the community that preaches succumbs to the very evil it seeks to resist. It is no easy matter to be poor as Jesus was poor, avoiding the romanticism of a poverty so radical that it becomes its own achievement, eluding the temptation to compromise poverty so artfully that one remains comfortable in the world while enjoying the consolations of the spiritual life. The most fatal greed is the one that appropriates the profits of two worlds, posing as pious while denying oneself no material advantage.

The point we wish to develop, however, is the relationship between worship and the Spirit. We suggest that of all the Church's activity, nothing is more genuine a bearer of its tradition or more apt to the testing of the Spirit than its liturgy. The Church develops more problems when it teaches formally than when it communicates liturgically.

It always comes as a disappointment to educators that people are profoundly moved by emotions and not by concepts. Western civilization is suffering the burden of its almost infinite number of rational conclusions. Even Catholic educators suppose that careful attention to theological writing and conciliar documents may produce liberated, perhaps even radical Catholics in the future. It is a mystifying but all too frequent phenomenon that students with liberal concepts are sometimes reactionary in their behavior. Man is motivated less by reason than we suppose. Experience moves people more often; and experience is more akin to emotion than to reason.

One of the most painful adjustments maturity demands is the acceptance of life as it is rather than as we had wanted it to be. Philosophers, theologians, and educators find the adjustment as necessary and

as unwelcome as anyone else. Philosophical idealists, religious fanatics, and educational theorists fret their talent away devising systems no one appreciates because the world is not where their theories had insisted it had to be.

Learning to accept the world as it is and improve it in real although modest ways is akin to a concept we expressed earlier, namely, managing poverty so that we resist both romanticism and compromise. Poverty is absolutely necessary for the granting of the Spirit, but poverty must be genuine before the Spirit is real. The problem with many reformers is their romanticism, their attachment to reforms as ends in themselves. They are similar to some people who practice poverty so that they may revel in their indigence. The problem with many reactionaries is their compromise, their desire to have the world remain as it supposedly always was even though they must eliminate people and facts to prove their point. They are like those whose poverty is a device to get the best of both worlds. Always self-righteous, they manage to sound pious as they destroy. They are the ecclesiastical loyalists and the civil patriots, blind to the pain of others and somehow always comfortable. They are the Pharisees who have no doubt because they have little faith.

Poverty is the central mystery of the Spirit. Poverty requires the surrender of liberalism and conservatism for a world that operates in less simple categories. The simplicity of the Spirit is not the simplicity of one-sided solutions to problems but the simplicity of love. Love always creates a two-sided view of the world, one that puts others at the center rather than maintaining the middle of the universe

for oneself. The Trinity shows that even God does not seize the center of reality for one person but reserves it for a Father and the Son who, from their poverty, allow the Spirit to proceed.

The liturgy is an experience of the Spirit. It is not as rational a venture as doctrine nor as directly didactic as a Council nor as easily defined as a disciplinary procedure. It is an experience of two-sidedness, one in which teacher and taught exchange roles throughout the process. Liturgy is only as successful as the degree of participation it achieves among all who celebrate.

One of the most important values in education is the creation of a spirit of poverty between teacher and taught. Jesus accomplished this by coming to serve rather than be served, by giving his life, by rejoicing in the growth of others rather than in his own advancement. A teacher is effective when he is committed to the enlightenment he brings rather than the authority he may have. But how does the Church bring about these realities? Jesus is no longer historically present; the Church is not a university. The most decisive means the Church has at its disposal is the liturgy. In the liturgy, the Spirit of Jesus is present in its most dramatic and least-defined form. The liturgy is an invitation to experience and participation.

We discussed symbols and ritual in earlier chapters. A symbol has meaning because two people have shared the same experience. This is why the symbols of one culture have little meaning for another. If two cultures undergo the same experience, they can share each other's symbols. The point behind arranging symbols in a ritualistic system is the

linking of many spiritual experiences so that their
full impact may become profound and lasting.

In order to experience something with other
people, we must enter into the mystery of poverty.
We must communicate with others in their need
from our need so that the present poverty of people
may be exceeded. The Eucharist is rich with the
mystery of poverty. It is instituted by the poor man
of Nazareth, the Jesus who has no home in which to
be born, the one who comes among his own and they
receive him not, the young man who has nowhere to
lay his head, the itinerant preacher who dies a criminal's death on an alien hill and is buried in a stranger's tomb. From his poverty Jesus creates liturgy.
The mystery of poverty extends even to his Sonship
with the Father. The Son is the one person of the
Trinity who becomes man because a son must be in
a situation of poverty before the Father who gives
him life. The son is most involved in the mystery of
poverty. The Eucharist is instituted by the poor man
of Nazareth, from Mary who had no material means
and from Joseph who is humble in his craft and
anonymous in his life. Throughout his ministry,
Jesus incarnationalizes poverty. He is deprived of the
support of the religious establishment of his day, denied the consolation of his own disciples in his hour
of extreme need, unable, it seems, even to reach his
Father from the cross.

The liturgy is a celebration of these many
themes, a reminder that God does not wish to be
isolated, a revelation of the emptiness out of which
life is made. To enter this liturgical experience, we
require a community, peace with the Church, forgiveness from God. At a liturgical celebration, we

form a circle of need so that we may create life and give life. We beg for the Spirit because we are trapped by the materialism of the world, the limitations of secular life, the suffocation of our own resources. Beggars for the Spirit, we plead for a presence not of this world and yet in it to save us from the world, so that we may live devotedly for the world.

The liturgy is for the wanderers in the wilderness of life who ask God to make a home for them in the hearts of others so that they will not be estranged from their brethren or deprived of God.

It is serious business, this liturgy we take at times so lightly. It is a call to God to break the barriers of our flesh and the confines of our hearts, the narrowness of our spirits and the inadequacy of our understanding. The liturgy asks God to make us poorer so that we might have no resources except love.

Celebrations of the liturgy sometimes fail because those who come to recall the poverty of Jesus are too full. Life can be given only when there is emptiness beforehand. A man cannot create life in the body of a woman who has already conceived life. A person cannot become a teacher for those who already know. A prophet cannot preach his message if the world does not perceive the dire situation in which it exists.

More than anything else the liturgy intends the gift of the Spirit. So long as there is a Spirit to empty the world of its sense of sufficiency, there will be hope for the world and love. The grace of the liturgy is the gift of one's own need, a need one senses because God is near. The liturgy is, therefore, a

priestly action. It is an action taken by a community
of the priesthood of believers with the offering of
their own emptiness and the sacrifice of their own
sufficiency.

We never draw near to people whose weakness
we do not perceive. A fruitful relationship begins
when the weakness of another prompts us to heal
and love, to sacrifice rather than take advantage.
The Incarnation was God's revelation of his
weakness, an invitation that we heal his humanity by
the love of our brothers. Some never saw the
weakness; others encountered only the strength of
God and feared or resisted. Some became aware of
the weakness and, taking advantage of his vulnerability, led him outside the city and crucified him in
poverty and pain. But some, realizing the weakness
of God, responded with their own poverty and, leav-
ing all, followed him. To these he gave the power of
becoming the sons and daughters of God.

The liturgy celebrates a God of simple gifts. It
proclaims a community of fragile words, the breaking of bread, the death of the Lord, the deficiency of
wine, the love of Jesus on our behalf. The liturgy
makes us conscious of our needs, our need for forgiveness and redemption, for mercy and brotherhood, for God and his only begotten Son.

It has been said that the strong know how to
live with their weakness. No one loves unless he succumbs in some way. This is true even of God who as
Father yields to the Son and as Spirit proceeds from
both. Perhaps this is the purpose of death. Unless at
some point we succumb completely, we cannot be
made to live forever. Just as Easter is created from
the desperate poverty of Jesus, so our resurrection

from the dead will be a victory of the vanquished.

The liturgy finds a place in the world where people are not ashamed to be poor; it creates moments in history when the poor prevail and the powerful are scattered in the conceit of their hearts. The liturgy is the song we sing in an alien land, a song of the disinherited and dispossessed who have chosen the Lord as their portion. This is the desert in which the Spirit flourishes, the aridity from which the fountains of living waters flow. The Spirit that created the world required the poverty of Jesus to be set free in the history of our lives. A community of poor believers has become a herald of the future and a harbinger of the Spirit. How strange and yet consistent!

9
GRACE

There is but one grace in life: the presence of another person. Grace happens when we bring life to one another. In the Trinity, each person is grace for the other; in religious experience we are graced with a presence no human event can equal. Grace is the quality of joy, the surprise, the yearning for communion, the peace that results from the nearness of those we were meant to be near. Grace, like life, does not happen in a vacuum; it is woven with the texture of concreteness.

God is not a vague endeavor. Jesus imparts the presence of God in the particulars of time and place that bring people together. Grace is the only healing experience people encounter because the heart can be healed by nothing other than personal presence. All other healing agents are superficial, meant to resolve a physical complication or an economic deficiency or a culturally induced, arbitrary problem. History witnesses to the fact that people may have excellent medical care, considerable affluence, every advantage a culture can offer and yet succumb to despair. The emptiness of the human heart can be filled by grace alone. Without the grace of others, it dies, regally perhaps and impressively, but it dies nonetheless.

The emptiness of contemporary life should never have occurred had we believed the rational predictions of the last century. This or that advantage or revolution, this or that social reform or economic program, this or that educational opportunity or therapeutic technique promised a redemption it never delivered. Sometimes even Christianity was swept up in the euphoria and supposed it had something to offer more significant than the creation of a healing community. Sometimes the Church became so enthused with its legal order and ecclesiastical structures, with the authority of a few leaders and the docility of the many, with an artificial orthodoxy on a peripheral point or with the ingenuity of a disciplinary procedure that it neglected the people whose hearts were starved for life.

The human heart, properly cared for, has its own capacity to create order out of chaos. Anarchy occurs when there is an absence of grace, emptiness, a fear that persons have gone away and only issues or reforms remain. Anarchy is the symptom of gracelessness. When people sense that things are coming apart, that the center no longer holds, they signify the loss of grace in their lives or in the heart of the era in which they live. Anarchy and anonymity are allied. One wants no order where there are no people to love; he chooses to be nameless because his name has no human meaning. In the void, one prefers secrecy or sabotage, desperate solutions and destructive alternatives.

Grace and courage are the reverse of anarchy and anonymity. Courage (which derives from the word "heart") is always required for personal presence. A coward is neither straightforward nor trans-

parent; he prefers darkness and deception. He comes into the Garden at night in the guise and greeting of friendship.

God names himself in the Scriptures as "I am Who am," "I am the one who is here." He chooses not to be nameless; he declares his presence, even his place in the universe ("I am with you"). The courage of God is tested in the Trinity where the encounter is so total that they form one reality despite the distinction. God is the one who shows his face. In the Incarnation, God is all light. There is no darkness in him. The Trinity is the paradigm for all courage, the source of all grace. God's courage becomes man in Jesus and brings human existence to its most radical vulnerability. The courage of Jesus is the exposure of his life to love, which leads to the cross and revelation. God is revealed decisively in the dying of Jesus because revelation is complete only when nothing is withheld. Since Jesus wanted this revelation continued forever, he gave us the Eucharist, created in courage, replete with such grace that even the fear of impending death and the fear of being forgotten are expressed.

Cowardice requires that one preserve himself at all costs. The coward withdraws lest he be injured. He forever hides his face, his identity, his name, his intentions. He protects himself even at the cost of other lives and reputations. He elicits trust from others as a weapon to be used against them. But the Eucharist emerges from the breaking of the bread and the willingness of Jesus not to spare even the breaking of his heart. It is courage in the darkness, when disciples run for cover, when an apostle denies lest he be injured. Jesus walks to his betrayer and

opens his arms to his captors. In him, there is no darkness. There is nothing to hide. The fear he experiences is not the fear of discovery but the fear that his love will be used to destroy him and to dishearten those who depend on him.

One of the most recurring descriptions of the Easter experiences in the New Testament is their transparency. Jesus is seen in a new light. This inspires John to begin his Gospel with the description of Jesus as the light of the entire world, the one in whom there was nothing to conceal, no energy for cowardice, only grace, only courage, only love. The darkness could not comprehend so much light, could not draw near such brightness without seeing its own obscurity disappear. A coward does not understand the courage of the brave anymore than a criminal knows what innocence is or what it must be like to live without suspicion.

The purity of Jesus is the purity of love, as open to the world as a flower that offers itself to the sun, as made for light as a pearl that loses its beauty in the darkness and gathers grace as it is illuminated. The images of light in the life of Jesus are abundant, concentrated, compressed. There is a star for his birth, light in the heavens, a bright cloud in the Jordan, a burning Mosaic glory in the Transfiguration, a noonday sun as he expires on the hill of the skulls. He rises with the dawn and sends fire on the earth with the gift of his Spirit. The brilliance of Pentecost overcomes the cowardice of the disciples and sends them courageously shouting in the streets of Jerusalem their desire to become a grace for those they love. There is no anonymity. They reveal their names and faces.

The Church begins its central liturgical service in the darkness of Easter night, near dawn, by igniting black coals and lighting the paschal candle. These symbols are striking in their significance. The coals lose their obscurity and are consumed by light as they become exposed to the air and the fire. The candle exhausts itself as it strains for the flame that extinguishes it even as it creates brilliance. There is courage in the Easter night that allows the darkness no deception. Nothing is hidden. It is a time to tell one's name and show one's face. It is a night for name-giving in the venerable liturgical tradition of the Church, the best of all seasons for baptism, the time to renew baptismal promises by speaking one's name in the congregation of believers. It is the night when Jesus becomes the Christ, when Simon becomes Peter. The light that bursts forth on this night will later transfigure Saul into Paul in a lightning flash. It is Easter night, a time that gathers together the burning fires of the Sinai desert and the pillar of flame that preceded the wandering Israelic community. It is a night of grace, of burning coals and prophetic speech, of tongues of fire and healed wounds. It is the night when the crimson suffering of the cross becomes the red glow of dawn, when wine once changed into the blood of Christ is changed again into the light of the Spirit. It is the night when men walk with no fear, when tears no longer blind, when sins no longer make the darkness appealing. It is a holy night, a night for Christmases and Easters, when angelic songs are sung and tombs are unsealed in the sunlight.

The Church this night becomes a chorus of song, inviting those who trust the light to hear the

bells and join hands. Christ comes only into a circle
of love. We know that a circle is broken if it has no
center or if anyone is absent. This is the night when
the center holds and when Christ becomes the focal
point of history.

People remain divided as long as they suspect
the other person is hiding something. The Christian
community is a shattered family because none of the
churches believes enough in each of its liturgies. We
have come to liturgical celebrations with our respective creeds and denominational fears, with vested in-
terests and hidden agendas, with closed hands and
suspicious hearts. The brokenness of the Christian
family is a sign of the insufficiency of our respective
liturgies, of our anxieties lest people corrupt the concepts and doctrines we suppose will save the Church
even if people cannot. We do not wish to become
simplistic. Every responsible believer knows that the
doctrine of Christianity must be safeguarded, that
we cannot become indifferent to orthodoxy or jeop-
ardize biblical faith with a naïveté that leads to
chaos. We insist, however, that too much energy has
been put into proper articulation of the faith. Orthodoxy does not emerge from doctrinal precision but
from the preparation of a community for proper per-
ception. We hear the truths we love and we love
more easily those who trust us and require our presence.

The world needs courage and grace. It does not
need concepts for its survival or structures for its
hope. It needs a community where courage is so radical that it dispenses with the power of the world, the
wealth of the world, the security of the world. This is
the message of Jesus, effectively present in the litur-

gy. There is no secular power in the breaking of the bread, no conquest in the drinking of wine, no affluence in the sharing of songs and light, no security in a circle of friends assembled to pray and beg God for Jesus, for another Easter, a new Christmas, one more dawn, and courage through the night. The Church becomes a liturgical community when it opens its door and greets its betrayers with love, when it fears neither its enemies nor its friends, when it relies on none of its resources or defenses but waits in the night, through an Advent evening and an Easter watch, for the light of the world.

Some people are unforgettable. They are those who loved us, those who revealed life by their openness. They are never the powerful who trust in their power or the wealthy who treasure their riches or the secure who forever close the shutters of their rooms and the windows of their soul lest the Spirit enter. Those we cannot forget always seem to have come into our lives too late and leave too quickly. They enchant us with their presence and their truth, their joy in life, their ability to see with open eyes and embrace with open arms. We close our hands when we are afraid or hostile. The clenched fist is a sign of terror or hatred. Those we cannot forget keep their hands open and their hearts vulnerable.

We observed in the beginning of this book that man has sought a presence from the beginning. Christianity encountered the presence fleetingly in the darkness and unfailingly at dawn. Christianity has been an effort to let others see what the apostles saw, to reveal a Christ with whom it is always good to be present. To do this, we have made symbols and sung songs; we have composed Gospels and remem-

bered words; we have learned names and devised rituals; we have preserved traditions and kept promises. We have not done this to burden the world with
formulas learned by rote or celebrations mechanized
by rubrics. We have acted so that the world may join
the circle and come out of the darkness. We have
done this so that the courage and grace of Christ
may become the focal point of a new beginning.

We have formed a circle so that we can see one
another's faces. A circle or a community makes hiding difficult. We have tried by all the energy of the
centuries and all the intensities of hope to make a
circle in the formlessness of the desert and to light a
fire at the center of the circle. People light their fires
in circles and sing songs in circles. The liturgy is a
search for a universal circle of grace and courage.

We noted as we developed this book that faith
led to liturgy and that Jesus was the name Christians
gave to the presence men have desired and loved,
lost and regained, pursued and questioned. The sacraments were the means by which the historical
events of the life of Jesus and the decisive events of
our personal history became a revelation and a communion of love. In the mystery of unspeakable poverty, we have sensed the Spirit and learned the language of love, been taught by God and humbled by
his need for us and his care for us. As a shepherd
who requires his sheep, the Lord of this immense
universe has pastured us with his presence and led us
home in the darkness, abiding with us until a new
day. He is the light and the voice we recognize. We
had sought him so long that our first encounter with
him established familiarity and friendship. The grace
and courage of the good shepherd, the fisher of Gali-

lee who sought men, the faithful Father who watched every day for us to walk out of the darkness back to his home, have been the most healing of all the experiences men have known.

One day Easter shall break upon the whole world. A large circle of love will become a new community. Christ will be born as he had not been born before, not for a few shepherds or a handful of Gentiles, not even for a band of disciples or a limited number of friends. Someday Christ will be born and his light will allow no further darkness. On that day we shall know all the names and name all our friends. We shall call Jesus "Savior" and he shall come as he always comes, simply, in the bread and wine we require for life and in the peace that makes all power pointless. We shall come to complete the circle, to make love out of liturgy one more time and to grace everyone. We shall become the sheep of a new Passover to whom God becomes the most faithful of all shepherds. In this final celebration we shall recognize him in the breaking of the bread and see each other's faces in the new wine he shares with us in the liturgy of heaven. No longer a stranger at our side, he shall set our hearts on fire and we shall die without fear because this time we shall be held forever in his arms and awake in the circle of his heart.